Teacher's Pet

by D. Jakobs
illustrated by Jim Talbot

SCHOLASTIC INC.

New York   Toronto   London   Auckland   Sydney
Mexico City   New Delhi   Hong Kong   Buenos Aires

ISBN-13: 978-0-545-03423-4
ISBN-10: 0-545-03423-X

Littlest Pet Shop © 2008 Hasbro
LITTLEST PET SHOP is a trademark of Hasbro and is used with permission.
© 2008 Hasbro. All Rights Reserved.

Lexile is a registered trademark of MetaMetrics, Inc.

Published by Scholastic Inc. SCHOLASTIC and associated logos are trademarks and/or registered trademarks of Scholastic Inc.

12 11 10 9 8 7 6 5   8 9 10 11 12/0

Printed in the U.S.A.
First printing, July 2008

It is the first day of school. This little pet wants to look her best. Which bow will she wear today?

The bell will ring soon. There is so much to talk about.

The pets are excited for school to begin.

It is time for yoga. That downward dog pose looks great.

Look at that perfect tree pose.
Yoga relaxes the pets.

This duck loves to swim.

This puppy really knows how to paddle.
Great job!

These puppies start learning tricks early.

First they learn to roll over. Then it is time to fetch.

The race is on! Gym class is fun when you love to run.

Who is going to finish first?

These cats and kittens learn how to dance.
They can stretch with grace, too.

Practice makes perfect in the gym.
It is a good thing practicing is so much fun.

The balance beam is tricky. It is important to stay focused.

Flying class is great! These pets are high in the sky.

This pet loves helping out. One day, she hopes to be a teacher, too.

It is time for lunch. The pets eat and talk.

It is always fun to share with friends!

After lunch, some pets jump rope.
Others play a game of tag.

Kickball is fun, too!

Art class can be messy. These pets like to paint.

These pets sing all the right notes.

They are practicing for a big concert.

The school dance team knows how to move.

These pets are hip and they can hop!

These pets meet after school. They are planning a school dance.

It will be a night to remember.

The first day of school has been great.
This school year is going to be the best yet!